Garden of Silica

IDA VITALE (Montevideo, Uruguay, 192⌐ ⌐ ⌐ ⌐ ⌐ ⌐ ⌐ ⌐ ⌐ ⌐ ⌐ the fundamental voices of Latin American literature. Her ⌐ ⌐ ⌐ encompasses poetry, essays, short stories, and translation. She studied humanities and taught literature in Uruguay until 1973, when the military dictatorship annihilated its society and culture. She lived exiled in Mexico from 1974 to 1984. Once democracy was reestablished, she returned to Uruguay, where she soon discovered that wounds caused by repression would not easily heal. Since 1989 she lives in Austin, Texas, USA. Vitale has authored some thirty books, among which poetry prevails. From her first collection *The Light of this Memory* (1949) to her most recent *Trema* (2005), her poetry constructs an intellectual, participative subject that relegates nationalism and even feminist ideologies to a second plane. Nevertheless, Vitale offers one of the most profound and provocative representations of feminine subjectivity in the Spanish language.

Earthworks Series
Series Editors: Katherine Hedeen, Gordon Henry Jr,
Janet McAdams & Víctor Rodríguez Núñez

KIMBERLY BLAESER: *Apprenticed to Justice*
JUAN CALZADILLA: *Journal with No Subject*
QWO-LI DRISKILL: *Walking with Ghosts*
HEID E. ERDRICH: *The Mother's Tongue*
JUAN GELMAN: *The Poems of Sidney West*
DIANE GLANCY: *Rooms: New and Selected Poems*
ALLISON ADELLE HEDGE COKE: *Blood Run*
ALLISON ADELLE HEDGE COKE (ed): *Effigies*
GORDON D. HENRY: *The Failure of Certain Charms
   and Other Disparate Signs of Life*
LEANNE HOWE: *Evidence of Red: Poems and Prose*
DEBORAH A. MIRANDA: *The Zen of La Llorona*
PHILLIP CARROLL MORGAN: *The Fork-in-the-Road Indian Poetry Store*
PHILIP RED EAGLE: *Red Earth: A Vietnam Warrior's Journey*
CARTER REVARD: *How the Songs Come Down: New and Selected Poems*
CAT RUIZ: *Stirring Up the Water*
RALPH SALISBURY: *Blind Pumper at the Well*
CHERYL SAVAGEAU: *Mother/Land*
JAMES THOMAS STEVENS: *A Bridge Dead in the Water*
IDA VITALE: *Garden of Silica*
GERALD VIZENOR: *Almost Ashore*

Garden of Silica

Ida Vitale

English versions by
Katherine Hedeen
& Víctor Rodríguez Núñez

London

PUBLISHED BY SALT PUBLISHING
Fourth Floor, 2 Tavistock Place, Bloomsbury, London WC1H 9RA United Kingdom

Salt Publishing 2010

Printed and bound in the United Kingdom by Lightning Source UK Ltd

Typeset in Swift 9.5 / 13

ISBN 978 1 84471 465 0 paperback

1 3 5 7 9 8 6 4 2

for Enrique

Contents

Acknowledgements   xi
Ida Vitale or the Brilliances of the Intellectual Subject   xiii

from EACH IN HIS NIGHT   1
   This World   3
   Daily Obligations   4

from LISTENER ERRANT   5
   Queen Sphinx   7
   Pallid Signs   8
   One Chooses   9
   Recreational   10
   Backroom   11

from GARDEN OF SILICA   13
   Tracing through Transparency   15
   Natural Fortunes   16
   Distance's Square   17
   Summer   18
   Against Time   19
   Past's Liquid   20
   The Dervish's Answer   21
   Perspective   22
   Homage to Magritte   23
   Nocturnal Wheel   24
   The Hunt, Infinite?   25
   Psalm   26
   Star's Passage   27
   Confirmation of Shadow   28
   At the Speed of Fear   29

The Blind Machine   30
Alameda   31
Garden of Silica   32
Zoon Politikon   33

from DREAMS OF CONSTANCY   35
Style   37
Justice   38
Composition with Symbols   39
Residue   40
Chaos   41
Efraín's Burial   42
Destiny   43
Rest   44
Story   45

from SEARCH FOR THE IMPOSSIBLE   47
Moth, Poem   49
Hummingbird   50
Rivers   51
Houses   52
The Day, A Labyrinth   53
Destinies   54
Midday Demon   55
Equation   56
Scarcely Concert   57
Small Kingdom   58
The Dark Table   59
Exiles   61
Still Canto   62
Cocoon   63
To Burn, To Quiet   64

The Lie   65
The Injured Man's Greeting   66
Botánica   67
Laurels   68
San Miniato   69

from REDUCTION OF THE INFINITE   71
    Parenthesis, Fragile Home   73
    Culture of Palimpsest   74
    Sums   75
    Slow Obstacles   76
    Salamanders' Mail   77
    Annunciation   79
    The Glory of Philitis   80
    To Arms   81
    Order of Angels   82
    Lunatic Solo, Legitimate Isolation 83

from BYOBU'S ABCs   85
    A Story   87
    Very Platonic Love   88
    Knots   89
    Anguish   90

from TREMA   91
    Task   93
    Calculated Error   94
    Arrows   95
    Last Night of Some Year   96
    On the Back of the Sky   97
    The Visible God   98
    If Blind   99

No Saga   100

Fortune   101

The Street   102

Bogota, 2001   104

New Certainties   105

Merry-Go-Round   106

Courtesies   107

Riches   109

On the Dark Porch   110

Return Trip   111

Perhaps an Explanation   112

Milan Café   113

Closing   114

Mining the Wall   115

Gratitude   116

Acknowledgements

The translators would like to gratefully acknowledge the poet Ida Vitale for her support of this project.

Acknowledgments

Ida Vitale or the Brilliances of the Intellectual Subject

Idea Vilariño complains that anthologies of Spanish American poetry have for too long "utterly ignored feminine writing," and that even "Juan Gustavo Cobo Borda's comprehensive collection mentions, among some seventy poets, only six women" (7).[1] Nonetheless, as Reneé Scott points out, "in the last twenty years one of the most significant occurrences in Spanish American literature has been the recognition of feminine discourse" (5).[2] Thus, the fact that Spanish America's traditional criticism has not paid enough attention to the splendid poetry of Ida Vitale (Montevideo, Uruguay, 1923), and above all in her native Uruguay, can—to a certain extent—be explained. However, what has no justification is that the region's feminist criticism, which should by definition correct the blunder, has been completely silent with regard to her case. Perhaps this is because she is a woman who, from both critical points of view, doesn't write like a woman ought to. In other words, by not prioritizing the construction of a feminine poetic subject this author challenges the old Spanish American canon as well as the new.

Every since adolescence, when she discovered Antonio Machado's poetry, Ida Vitale has written verses. Her first poem, a sonnet, was published in the journal, *Hiperión*, in September 1942. That same year she began her studies, first in Law and later in Humanities, at the Universidad de la República in Montevideo, but never graduated. One of her professors was the Spanish writer José Bergamín, exiled then in Uruguay, whose teaching influenced her early poetry. Thanks to his recommendations she reclaimed the German and French Romantics and read Octavio Paz and María Zambrano. When Juan Ramón Jiménez passed through Montevideo in 1948, "he took along some of her poems and included them in *Presentación de la poesía hispanoamericana joven*, an anthology published in Buenos Aires, in which two Uruguayan women writers are present: Idea Vilariño and Ida Vitale" (Caballé 531–32).[3] Along with Ángel Rama, José Pedro Díaz, and Vilariño, among others, she founded the cultural journal *Clinamen* (1947–1948). And the book, *La luz de esta memoria* (Montevideo: La Galatea, 1949), a notably solid first effort, appeared.

Hugo Verani argues that Ida Vitale is "an isolated and exceptional figure among the poets of her generation in Uruguay" (569), but this is only half true.[4] She belongs, not only for chronological reasons, to the so-called Critical Generation (or the Generation of '39, or '40, or '45). Graciela Mántaras Loedel affirms that this group, "belligerent and parricidal, began around 1939. It favored an exigent, rigorous, multi-spanning critical exercise and ended up founding a new table of values. It became current with the century's literary innovations and proceeded to revise the cultural past to equip itself with a 'useful tradition'" (7–8).[5] All this activity, according to Carlos Real de Azúa, "had no other choice but to lead to a total, complete rupture [. . .] from what was considered to be around 1945 or 1950 official literature or historiography, laden with rhetoric and conformism, [. . .] stylized by a purely decorative notion of intellectual function" (qtd. in Paternain 81-82).[6] Along with Vitale, the major poets of this generation are, according to Mántaras Loedel, "Vilariño (1920), Mario Benedetti (1920), Amanda Berenguer (1921), Gladys Castelvecchi (1922), [. . .] Sarandy Cabrera (1923), Carlos Brandy (1923) and Humberto Megget (1926–1951)" (7–8).

What is certain is that Ida Vitale actively participated in her generation's cultural task. She collaborated with its most emblematic vehicle of expression, the weekly *Marcha*; and also with the journals *Asir* and *La Licorne*, and the daily newspapers *El País* and *Época*. She made various formative trips: France (1955–56), where she traveled on scholarship; Cuba (1964 and 1967), where she was a judge for the Casa de las Américas Prize and participated in the "Encuentro con Rubén Darío"; and the Soviet Union (1965). Uruguay was not isolated from the convulsive process unleashed by the Cuban Revolution beginning in 1959, which in the opinion of Benedetti, "served to accelerate a political (in the most civic sense of the word) reintegration in writers who had up until that point taken cover behind their erudition or fantasy" (35).[7] Nevertheless, Vitale did not align herself with any political party or aesthetic trend. New poetry collections appeared: *Palabra dada* (Montevideo: La Galatea, 1953), *Cada uno en su noche* [*Each in His Night*] (Montevideo: Alfa, 1960), and *Oidor andante* [*Listener Errant*] (Montevideo: Arca, 1972).

These decisive years for Ida Vitale's development as a poet are characterized, according to Rama, by a process of "the decomposition of liberalism, produced in the country that had illusorily perfected a liberal economy and society, sponsored by England and cultured by France" (223).[8] Significantly, the critic points out that the period's intellectuals were "in the vast majority ideological gravediggers of Uruguay's liberal regimen" (223). This preeminence of intellectual function is singular, as few times had the contribution "to consciousness raising, to the explanation of reality, to the formation of new generations, to training for change, to the acquisition of indispensable moral values in order to confront the political and economic degradation of the reigning oligarchy in power" been so relevant (217–18). Rama concludes that with this effort poetry functioned "like the vanguard in motion, incessantly announcing new discoveries, areas of reality still unknown, spiritual states barely glimpsed at within society" (238).

It can be affirmed then that Ida Vitale's poetry is at the very center of her generation's mission: the construction of a participative intellectual subject. This relegates others, like a national subject, or in this author's specific case, a feminine subject, to a second plane. The latter is particularly sensitive because in Uruguayan contemporary poetry, as Washington Benavides recognizes, there has been an absolutely exceptional "feminine poetic prevalence" (8).[9] In that country of "an abundant middle class that encouraged the cultivation of literature, for more than one hundred years women have created a rich, varied literary discourse" (Scott 5). The standouts of this tradition are the poets Delmira Agustini (1886–1914), Juana de Ibarbourou (1892–1979) and Sara de Ibáñez (1909–1971); the narrator Armonía Somers (1914–1994); the already mentioned members of the Critical Generation; and among other contemporary writers, the poet and narrator Cristina Peri Rossi (1941). Jorge Oscar Pickenhayn recognizes in Uruguayan poetry "more than sixty women's names, whose resonance is confirmed by undeniable merits" (7).[10]

On June 27, 1973 a coup d'état took place in Uruguay and the next year Ida Vitale went into exile in Mexico. There she lived for a decade, easily assimilating to the country's cultural activities, and collaborating with journals like *Plural* and *Vuelta* and newspapers like *El Sol* and *Unomásuno*. She published a new poetry collection, *Jardín de sílice [Garden of Silica]* (Caracas: Monte Ávila, 1980), and the anthologies *Fieles* (Mexico: El Mendrugo, 1977; Mexico: UNAM, 1982) and *Entresaca* (Mexico: Oasis, 1984). In sum, hers was "a beneficial exile" (Verani 568). In 1985, the military dictatorship defeated, she returned to Uruguay, where she remained until 1989. She wrote then for the weekly *Jacque* and became a member of the editorial boards of the journals *Poética* and *Maldoror*. In 1990 she moved to Austin, Texas, from where she collaborated with the journals *Posdata* and *Letras Libres*. Vitale has assumed her wanderings as a vital attitude and today divides her time between the United States, Uruguay and Mexico. Her poetry has multiplied in the last decades: *Sueños de la constancia [Dreams of Constancy]* (Mexico: FCE, 1988 and 1994), *Procura de lo imposible [Search for the Impossible]* (Mexico: FCE, 1998), *Reducción del infinito [Reduction of the Infinite]* (Barcelona: Tusquets, 2002), *El ABC de Byobu [Byobu's ABCs]* (Mexico: Taller Ditoria, 2004; Madrid: Adama Ramada, 2005) and *Trema* (Valencia: Pre-Textos, 2005).[11]

Throughout Ida Vitale's poetry is manifested the incompatibility between the construction of an intellectual subject and realism. It is not that we are before an idealist aesthetic that denies the existence of objective reality. Alejandro Paternain asserts that, as in the case of other authors from the Critical Generation, for our poet, "the closed circle of subjectivity [. . .] has opened to the world and the world has entered it, transforming it, renovating the senses and extending the reach of a sensibility that now corresponds with the sensibility of everyone" (41). For this reason Vitale not only offers us a testimony of her individuality; as Verani confirms, she "is the least autobiographical of modern Uruguayan poets [. . .], her poetry is neither a means of describing concrete experiences nor a vehicle for self-expression" (567). Ultimately, she is "a writer who rejects the notion of mimesis, of literature as simian imitation or representation of the concrete world" (Verani 568). Consequently, her poetry seeks a balance between objectivity and subjectivity; it "is concerned with the external world as well as with the inner world" (Verani 572).

Ida Vitale's intellectual subject places, accordingly, intellectual capacity above that of sentimentality. Thus, this poetry, radically at the margins of romanticism, "allows us to approach its powerful, serene anguish without flaunting its sentimentalism" (Paternain 38). This is reaffirmed by the fact that "[t]hese poems express a perspective that transcends her personal universe to embrace widely shared emotions" (Verani 569). They also appeal, as Anna Caballé shows, to "demistifying irony. [. . .] Suspecting certainties and definitions, she prefers to create problems and to dissent, point out cracks in which to withdraw from what is imposed upon her" (531). It should not be strange then that her message is implicit, requiring an active reader, a participant in the process of creation that is "more suggestive than representative" (Verani 567). This does not mean that Vitale is "deliberately obscure, for the reader can understand her poetry perfectly well on a superficial level. Complex themes are presented in a condensed form, masterfully captured in both their materiality and their mystery, their directness and their abstraction" (Verani 569).

By placing the intellectual subject at the forefront, Ida Vitale's poetry centers on representation itself; it not only attempts to make the referent visible but also the sign. Rafael Courtoisie confirms that our poet is always "attentive to words because they are a limit and they lie as well, yet their intensity, their very risk becomes a condition of life" (204).[12] Related to this practice is, as Antonio Mellis shows, "a growing process of the 'wearing down' of language" (qtd. in Rela 173–74).[13] There is an obvious awareness of the "power of language to suggest hidden states of mind without expressing them directly and, more important, [of] her ability to attain the greatest intensity of expression" (Verani 569). As the author herself affirms, "the world is full of people who are too satisfied. It must be known that one can always go further. And most of all, not accept that language says everything. What is said is a specter, a phantom of something else" (García Pinto 263).[14] The present anthology attempts to give an account of the usefulness and beauty of such an endeavor.

KATHERINE HEDEEN and VÍCTOR RODRÍGUEZ NÚÑEZ
Gambier, August 13, 2008

Notes

1   Vilariño, Idea, ed. and intro. *Antología poética de mujeres hispanoamericanas: Siglo XX*. Montevideo: Banda Oriental, 2001. Cobo Borda, Juan Gustavo, ed. and intro. *Antología de la poesía hispanoamericana*. Mexico: FCE, 1985. With regard to the topic, see Rodríguez Padrón, Jorge. *El barco de la luna: Clave femenina de la poesía hispanoamericana*. Caracas: Fundación para la Cultura Urbana, 2005.

2   Scott, Renée. *Escritoras uruguayas: Una antología crítica*. Montevideo: Trilce, 2002.

3   Caballé, Anna, ed. *Lo mío es escribir: La vida escrita por las mujeres, I*. Intro. Alicia Redondo and Fernando Aínsa. Barcelona: Lumen, 2004.

4   Verani, Hugo J. "Ida Vitale." *Latin American Writers. Supplement I*. Ed. Carlos A. Solé and Klaus Müller-Bergh. New York: Scribner, 2001. 567–79.

5   Mántaras Loedel, Graciela. "Introducción."*Contra el silencio: Poesía uruguaya 1973–1988*. Ed. and intro. Mántaras Loedel. Montevideo: Tupac Amaru, 1989.

6   Paternain, Alejandro. "36 años de poesía uruguaya (1930–1966)." *36 años de poesía uruguaya: Antología*. Ed. and intro. Paternain. Montevideo: Alfa, 1967. 18–64.

7   Benedetti, Mario. "La literatura uruguaya cambia de voz." *Literatura uruguaya: Siglo XX*. Barcelona: Seix Barral, 1997. 11–20. Benedetti adds that the Cuban Revolution "also served as a way for many to feel the necessity of a personal commitment (although this did not mean subjecting their work to inspiration and the ups and downs of a given political party). They were decidedly unwavering in risking their jobs, their careers and even maintaining a healthy distance from police squads. Finally, it served so that an external, apparently distant theme could become a national claim, and above all, so that the topic of Latin America finally penetrated our world, our people and also our cultural life, which had always suffered from an almost hypnotic dependence on Europe" (35).

8   Rama, Ángel. "Uruguay: La Generación Crítica (1939–1969)." *La crítica de la cultura en América Latina*. Ed. and intro. Saúl Sosnowski and Tomás Eloy Martínez. Caracas: Biblioteca Ayacucho, 1985. 217–40.

9   Benavides, Washington. *Mujeres: Las mejores poetas uruguayas del siglo XX*. Montevideo: Instituto Nacional del Libro, 1993.

10 Pickenhayn, Jorge Oscar. *Voces femeninas en la poesía de Uruguay*. Buenos Aires: Plus Ultra, 1999. The most rigourous account of this singular phenomena is Benavides' anthology, which includes works by María Eugenia Vaz Ferreira (1875–1924), Agustini, de Ibarbourou, Selva Márquez (1904–1981), Esther de Cáceres (1903–1971), Clara Silva (1905–1976), de Ibáñez, Vilariño, Berenguer, Vitale, Castelvecchi, Matilde Bianchi (1932), Nancy Bacelo (1931), Marosa di Giorgio (1932–2004), Circe Maia (1932), Peri

Rossi, Tatiana Oroño (1947), Cristina Carneiro (1948), and Silvia Guerra (1961). In other anthologies of Uruguayan poetry appear works by Petrona Rosende de la Sierra (1787–1863), Luisa Luisi (1883–1940), María Adela Bonavita (1900–1934), Sarah Bollo (1904–1987), Blanca Luz Brum (1905–1985), María Elena Muñoz (1905-1964), Susana Soca (1906-1959), Estrella Genta (1917–1979), Orfila Bardesio (1922), Silvia Herrera (1922), Dora Isella Russell (1925–1990), Selva Casal (1927), María Esther Cantonnet (1933), Suleika Ibáñez (1937), and Silvia Riestra (1958).

11 With respect to prose, Vitale has published the singular books *Léxico de afinidades* (Mexico: Vuelta, 1994), *Donde vuela el camaleón* (Montevideo: Vintén, 1996; Mexico: Sin Nombre, 2000), and *De plantas y animales: Acercamientos literarios* (Mexico: Paidós, 2003). She is also a distinguished critic and translator. She has written illuminating essays on Uruguayan poetry from the '20s and the works of her fellow Uruguayans Agustini, Felisberto Hernández, and Enrique Casaravilla Lemos. Latin American poets who have received her critical attention are Pablo Neruda, Nicanor Parra, Alberto Girri, Enrique Molina, Olga Orozco, Octavio Paz, Eliseo Diego, Gonzalo Rojas, Carlos Germán Belli, Rafael Cadenas, Roque Dalton, and José Emilio Pacheco. Additionally, she has translated works from French (Jean Dubois, Guillaume Apollinaire, Gastón Bachelard, Jules Supervielle, Simone de Beauvoir, and Emil Cioran), Italian (Luigi Pirandello, Massimo Bontempelli, Salvatore Quasimodo, Pier Paolo Pasolini, and Eugenio Montale), and English (Djuna Barnes, John Osborne, and John Synge).

12 Courtoisie, Rafael: "Ida Vitale (1923)." Benavides 201–4.

13 Rela, Walter. *Poesía uruguaya, siglo 20: Antología*. Montevideo: Alfar, 1994.

14 García Pinto, Magdalena. "Entrevista con Ida Vitale en México, 21 de julio, 1982." *Historias íntimas: Conversaciones con diez escritoras latinoamericanas*. Hanover [NH]: Ediciones del Norte, 1988. 253–81.

from *Each in His Night*

This World

Only I accept this illuminated world
certain, inconstant, mine.
Only I exalt its eternal labyrinth
and its safe glow, although it may be veiled.
Awake or among dreams
I walk its grave earth
and it is its patience in me
flowering.
It has a deaf circle,
limbo perhaps,
where blindly I await
rain, fire
unleashed.
At times its light changes,
is hell;
at times, rarely,
paradise.
Someone could perhaps
half open doors,
see beyond
promises, successions.
Only I in it live,
await it
and there is sufficient wonder.
In it I am,
remain,
would be reborn.

Daily Obligations

Remember the bread,
don't forget that dark wax
you must apply to the wood,
or the garnishing cinnamon,
or other necessary spices.
Run, correct, watch over,
verify each domestic ritual.
Keeping to salt, honey,
flour, useless wine,
simply trample the idle inclination,
your body's burning howl.
Pass, through this same threaded needle,
evening after evening,
between one fabric and another,
the bittersweet drowsiness,
the portions of destroyed sky.
And always may in your hands a ball of wool
endlessly unwind
like the turns in another labyrinth.

But don't think,
                    don't endeavor,
                                weave.
To memorize
look for favor among myths
is worth little,
You are Ariadne with no ransom
nor constellation for a crown.

from *Listener Errant*

Queen Sphinx

Standing on the serpent's box,
the queen, lifted by angels
or demons, goes behind sorcery.
A trail of pins has opened for her
so she may dance on their tips
and from behind a sword protects or slays her.
This century sets fire to her daily forests
of prohibited birds
and closes the scandal of her aimless travels.
Will she offer to die, a scorpion surrounded by dark enemies
or only to be covered with thorns,
with stings?
I trust she will maintain her scepter of madness,
gunpowder capable of bursting
the sufficient image of the world.

Pallid Signs

The bread died in the cupboard,
the milk, among jars
I forgot in the sun,
and plants I alternately
fed and abandoned, once again,
little by little, became soil.
Ants dress the sieged
patterns on tables.
Windows have sprouted free will,
they abhor light, change the scenery.
I don't know what winds come
from the worst thorn of some rose
winds snapping take away handkerchiefs,
constant cotton torn.
The gravest signs
—a Semmelweiss would say—
are puerperal fevers heated by
unexpected births.

One Chooses

Decimated, bleeding,
cut into as many parts
as dreams,
I want,
nonetheless,
this and no other way
to live;
this and no other way to die;
this shock
and no more the habitual
somnolence.
As a shadow of oneself
or violent lit match.
There is no alternative,
no more sign of identification.
No other death.
No greater life.

Recreational

Supposing we are at the bottom
of an imaginary well;
that this well has height,
curb, beyond sky
for someone who can reach it;
and assuming
its content
is rigid hopes,
guess the time
it will take
for whoever is
in its deepest part
to get to the top.

Formulate the answer
in viable dreams,
labyrinth ends,
volatile illusions.
Calculate as well
the lost energy
each time bottom once more
is touched.

Backroom

Montevideo's rapid skies,
layers of gold and laurel,
hauled by the highest net,
tepid lilacs sluggish
quotients of their multiplied light
pass and envelope us
and we are occupied by their loveliness,
like fingers play
among the sands holding
eternity in what we don't think.
Meanwhile, the pegasus danger
neighs ferociously.

from *Garden of Silica*

Tracing through Transparency

Sharp afternoon
abundant with firm attempts
—trumpet, telegram, shreds of Girondo—
reserves among its drupes, sadness.
Autumn forebodes movement
moves omens,
wastes its splendid veils
on dark rituals.
All nettles,
hieroglyphic ashes persist.
Only love detains
swift walls,
          postpones
collapse.
Through transparency
               you see the fire
devour
    the tallest barks
in the climbing gardens.
A warble
       terse compass, survives.

Natural Fortunes

Against presumptions, sun persists,
outside, not in,
glowing shapeless not guiding.
Other days its light is a lament,
a soft chatter.
          Almost as if we were
moss or herbs from kernels or fruit trees
the second day of creation.
As if the end of paradise were a sham.

Distance's Square

No matter that you are
on summer's stage,
the center of its challenges.
Far from its fires
alone you walk
between snow statues,
along the stones of Alejandro's
bridge,
      infinite.
You see yourself walk,
looking as ice curdles
in ephemeral islands,
the river runs below,
it yokes at a point
far from here
         what here?—
among new shores.

Lightning is unspeakable.
Return then in the opposite direction,
recuperate uses and customs,
sea,
     dead sand,
     this clarity,
          while you are able.
But preserve in your blood
           like a fish
the sweet clash of distance.

Summer

Everything is blue,
    what isn't green
        and burns,
            I.N.R.I.
igne natura renovatur integra—
in this grave oil of summer;
the one who weighs birds' journey falls
and blasphemes the flightless bird,
verbal excrescence falls =
              prophecy = trophy,
jewel on the same old skin.

Whoever sits at the shore of things
glows of things without shores.

Against Time

There, in the indecisiveness leading
to the dead woman's posthumous room
they placed the lily of the valley's snow.
I waited silently
to see if it would sing meanings
a lute that in the nakedness of infancy
was going to tell stories without safeguard,
offer an omen's trepidation.
But it was a drop of silence,
so we would quiet,
                    simply
sumptuously.
Its music,
                constellation of white,
diamond,
                placid silver bell,
still plays transparently,
above, against time,
among lights.

Past's Liquid

Absolute cistern.
                    Some star.
Unfathomable oil.
Through the sign's hollow I cross
brief tongues of radiance,
                            an infinite night.
A magnetic well burns.
Where does it stop this well
                                carbonized to black?
Is there a guarantee at the bottom,
                         a sentence
at the moment of arrival?
Where?
Near a resplendent final food
or new ovary?
Question or honor always present.
Will I again see what wasn't?
From not being to not being
a thread
—silk or steel only the end knows—
tangles vanished steps.
Each laceration,
                   each trophy
remain as the fern
in stone's heart,
                invisible,
until the strike fractures and undresses it.

The Dervish's Answer

Perhaps
knowledge consists
of distance if something vibrates
our movement
(because the horrible spider
falls over its victim)
to see,
      reflected like a star,
distant reality.

In this way
the situation flowers before our eyes
or loses
        one by one
            its petals—
like a species seen
for the first time.
And we will judge sadly,
               vain mending
that nothing repairs,
this trivial sketch of our gesture,
improbable amulet
against the emigration of certainties.

Perspective

In the foreground pleats,
jewels, faces
                    fleur-de-lised riders
usurp with human news
the veil of the cloud in the sky,
the distant cypress, the hills,
the rivers like ribbons at the end of a party.

Toward the perspective,
the surface becomes transparent,
enameled design that pleasures the eye,
table of temptations
where the gaze runs fast
to the invisible fountain
of the seen.

A man searches for doors toward
eluding the contingency
that spies from this side of the cloth,
pledged to win a place
the onager would not prefer
nor terrors live;
he calls behind that infinite,
                              attempts,
sliding hopeful lenses,
to discover and bring nearer
what is hidden,
what must be sustaining the miracle.
And only finds
the limit once again
and the inquiry.

Homage to Magritte

From the sky a rider
gallops towards forests,
an Amazon
                    crosses woods
crossing her.
The key to dreams
is the key to fields is
the memory of every journey is
metaphysical territories.   —leaf ?

From the petiole of a leave come
stratagems in sequence to dodge fears,
                    faithful similes,
                    approximations of candor
                    and of wet,
                              laborious fear,

like a lion flying among laurels and trumpets,
                    a boulder raises in flight its castle,
                    an apple invades the reading room;
what in our memory tantalizes
covers the skies with storms,
crumbles mysterious barricades
with a light all discernment.
Fertile eyes
create processional days,
afternoons filtrating
in the visible world
                    pavilions
of upset space.

Magritte clouds will always be swift.

Nocturnal Wheel

Here
—desert, labyrinth—
confronted with papers changing
the instant you look at them,
among books limiting each page
with death,
you hear the chorus of screams for help
your struggle repeated
                              sign by sign
against the eternal viper.
Secret sister,
hurls hopeful cords,
faithful scales
                    with precise knots,
plants and watches over the bean that
from its vertiginous kernel
reaches the sky.
Is it of use?
              Afterwards,
there is always fatigue,
                              jungle
to hide from the furious poison.

The Hunt, Infinite?

Islands:
        so much clearness is mystery.
Tunnels cross them,
dynamited labyrinths
to be reborn of themselves,
mazes with bull and dreams
and insatiable Theseus from the myth
and Ariadne who one day begins
the always
            eternal
reading of truth
              that
fabled,
        circular in the waters escapes,
fixed to the shore of a beginning,
of a closed infinite closed.

Psalm

Praise what you do not know
because of your hope
and even your look of today
                              believer
in the beauty that many disdain:
praise it as inconceivable,
as the constancy of its absurd dispositions.
Your journey's route
                         briefly infinite
traces a drawing only you do not understand,
but do not rise up;
in the raucous vacuum of its center
you will fall
                  transmutable seed
when beauty and hope
in reverie
                  pass on.

Star's Passage

If that past
flying from different starting points
became a serene waltz
if fragment's fascination
magic mountain's blow
fulminating rooftops
could harmonize
with tribulations' triumph
lute's drop
       and then
nights discoveries ends
all the torrent of newly wedded metamorphoses
when together we would gather the confusion
that numbers the years
happy occasions yoked
perhaps fear
       sorrow
even an eternal twilight
final flowers.

Confirmation of Shadow

Lizards in the darkness,
private prisoners
of running toward the sun,
they pile up, one body over another,
scales of a sinuous,
                    long
different reptile.
Taciturn thoughts,
no less incapable
of lighting their own fire,
are linked,
                achieve
a perseverant succession,
useless, rough
and calm,
they barely confirm shadow,
to govern a space without light of its own.

At the Speed of Fear

At times it has the color
of an afternoon at a park,
the melancholy that always
accompanies beauty.
It awaits at the perfect distance.
At times it seems to be so close,
behind the window,
willing to break the glass
isolating me.
I still know how to measure the speed
of its step,
the time of its distractions.
I am its fixed, waning limit.

The Blind Machine

You are getting nearer to the place
                                    where
one dies best;
                    there
a dark sun illuminates
cold.
Unhurried hands
                    succumb
to the other gravity
where definitively to fall
toward solitude.
Together all the tears
lead to where
cathedralic night
                    bursts.

Alameda

Against invisible stars
—their memory like
a fresh path in the night—,
against their annihilated glow,
the false, radiant
net of brilliances
lit from so high walls.
One could error like in dreams.
Suddenly,
out of garden's dark splendor,
almost at your feet,
ran the cold, real
                    rat,
sharper than today,
stubbornly blurred.

Garden of Silica

Si tanto falta es que nada tuvimos.
— GABRIELA MISTRAL

Now
one must pay time's consumption,
without hindrance,
                    the ecstasy spent
in walking through a garden of silica.
We plough once again the same furrow
for misfortune's fertility,
and the letter,
                    the silence
enter with blood.

Years to graze words like dark pastures
will come,
put to blaze small salamanders,
all exorcisms,
scarce memorials where there was open air,
no longer a common place,
                        that no one
in the fear of crossroads
dreams or reads.

Roving boxcars cross
                    toward
a past pulverizing roots,
polishing sorrow and bidding us farewell.

Zoon Politikon

Il n'y a de paix qu'au-dessus des
serpents de la terre.
           — MAX JACOB

You would like to write at the margins of combustions
    and shivers,
    machine-gunning weeds
        and testimonies of the failure of all magic,
    remedying gnawed quicksilver so
           from the other side of the mirror one arrives
           to gardens without storm or astuteness,
           where the circular tea and close far away friends
           await.
You would like to change swamps to springs of clean
           water-cress,
    hoist history,
    slithering web where you trip
    and are covered with bruised omens.

Yet you continue through suffocating sands to no end,
    to run aground in the promised horror.
    Your back, sad sign,
    reveres tablets dictated among
        thunder and violence.

You would like to be born in the age of reason.

from *Dreams of Constancy*

Style

The vertigo of others'
corporations feathered
for parties or jungle rage
passes.
The dialect ends.
Meanwhile, the tongue's deep
basting reads

in diminutive jasmine or sand,
leaves the tempting boil,
and imagines the simple
glittering
foam of the last wave.

And fits once again
in the condyle
in the exactness
of fatality.

Justice

The farmer sleeps on a mattress of hay.
The fisher of sponges rests
on his softened harvest.
Will you sleep, lightly floating
on written paper?

Composition with Symbols

A basket filled with snow
and three red apples,
a cloud with its crests to the wind,
a blue man descending
a pine's royal stairway,
a tree offering mirrors
instead of bitter fruit,
an avenue of poplars
changing to swords,
two cups with two suns within
overturned by a charcoal octopus,
death among mirrors
unending, alliterative.
Mute eyes see it.
Blind lips attempt to fix
such drifting.

Residue

Whether life is short or long, all
we live is reduced
to a gray residue in our memory.

Of the old journey remain
the enigmatic coins
claiming false value.

From memory only a
a vague dust and perfume rise.
Could it be poetry?

Chaos

Chaos
satanic and free,
kingdom of the I,
burns cupboards
        of humid glories,
fire gloriously fatuous.

Efraín's Burial

All glory
            the earth hastens
silence
sun
blue
and clouds.
In an air without fraud
birds sing
            a brief cavatina.
And the Woman laid out
                        entranced keeps vigil.

You continue on
the mysterious journey.
There is no more Juárez-Loreto,
                        seductions.

You will arrive
            no longer hurried
to the station you were preparing.

Above
      we are quiet
who knows where we will go.

Destiny

They will have offered you their hand,
condoned the debt,
served,
as if it were possible to choose now,
paralysis or dreams.
At this hour carnivorous gods
will have abandoned the forest;
cunning, they have let you go
so you descend toward the circle,
so you error
and say: *why*,
so while seeing you become blind,
and with all the music within your reach
you fill with clumsy,
sad wax, your ears.

Rest

Being feather after feather
these wings lose
their malicious flight,
perform in less and less air,
linger
in disturbing stillness.
Bit after bit
wind has carried away
so much fragment from skin
to dust,
from light to shadow,
from riddle to oblivion,
that the open breadth is false now,
in a day of constant wolves
the eagle's sham
you attempted.
Looking at them folded
you slowly begin to walk.

Story

We ascended the long stairway running.
We barely saw possible
lateral details,
surprises of a window
open to the world behind the glass,
reflections, sediments
of who had ascended before.
We rapidly crossed
the landing's useless gap,
less than natural roses abandoned,
the same old lashes
sky blind
to its indelible way.
We ascended, ascended
like always
only toward less and less light,
toward deeper well.

from *Search for the Impossible*

Moth, Poem

In the air was
imprecise, tenuous, the poem.
Imprecise as well
the moth arrived,
not beautiful or ominous,
to get lost among folding screens of paper.
The frayed, weak ribbon of words
dissipated with it.
Will both return?
Perhaps, in a moment of darkness,
when I no longer want to write
something more foreboding
than that hidden moth
avoiding light, as the Fates.

Hummingbird

A bright spot vibrating,
a brief sun on the fence,
a zz zz releasing to the air
its dangerous secret

and now the flower diminishes
before the feather's wonder
emerging, dazzling and fleeing
and I can only reach it due to

a stubborn number of years, where
spell's prisoner, I follow in vain
the miraculous dexterity
that holds it in my hand

and then for a moment
to feel how the world beats.

Rivers

Distant, on this riverbank,
you often imagine yourself distant,
on the banks of another river,
imagining yourself on this bank
awaiting
      mysterious rivers
to descend.

Houses

Living rooms in shadow, blind, lone houses,
patiently watch us leave,
burden us with their stillness,
suspended in thresholds they wait.
They know we always return to them,
to the silo their space signifies,
more than the city itself.

(But what night do we return? How?
To be ghosts, to be diligently the adventitious,
ambling without support?)

At times, with our backs turned they fall.
                                    Later,
a connect-the-dots
                    the absent balcony hangs
and visions appear but they no longer watch us.

The Day, A Labyrinth

The day, a labyrinth
where you only have light
                a few moments.

You go to the dizzying table,
look at papers,
            crumpled seas,
confused letters,
               foliage from another autumn,
the register of the day,
              the labyrinth
where you only had light
            a few moments.

Destinies

Patience may be the virtue of the adulterated
who look into the blind, blinding well.
There the shadow of the identical awaits
like a purple tapestry
hung for the crime.
Inaccessible gestures, persuasive words
reproach the only blame they do not have,
time.

Midday Demon

February burns, burns
and the midday demon
wags his tail toward the nap
and it is difficult to think.
We barely go by margins
of images.

A dagger can be a dagger
of the mind, there frozen
claw or dagger,
stain at every moment
of the mind,
digging into the heart.

To create then mists, meadows,
blackbirds,
              mind's seas,
as provisional as those real,
to save February,
frighten its demon.

Equation

Arm a word in the wolf's mouth
and the word bites.

In the sky's shifting brilliance
toward sunset,
quietly running ashore, becoming glow,
is Venus:
        lamb incandescent.

Scarcely Concert

The oboe's many sophistries,
so many spiral turns toward the cupola
of a sky no one disputes
ivy's ostentations
in the afternoon's last sun—
and tumbles toward the violoncello's docile sand,
do not hinder the unassailable reality:
the continuous bass perseveres.

Here a concert
               and nothing more.

Small Kingdom

A bird
whistling in defense of its branch
or the minimal rainbow,
sprinkling's peacock tail
do not suffice.

A book,
the silence where one manages
to transform something to gold
or what is a burden,
                         almost thought
do not suffice.

Your indolence is as ancient
as some inconclusive pages
and just this is your kingdom.

The Dark Table

I

At last the circular table,
yet, flickering from nonsense, the candlelight.
Outside, untamed,
others' foliage cuts
level sandy grounds.
It will always be another place,
soil,
      sky
and the down of your insufficient chest.
Gardens will die far from you
because at the edge of this dark table
dark well without answers you look
and see another past
and you will see another death.

II

Sadness brings twilight
—North wind interlude—
trivial tragedy brings
—incomplete light upon jumping
night is a trampoline,
like this table, dark—
shattered starless.
We are emptied in abundance.
And it is an opaque sliding
what we gild life.
And they have destroyed the last
trees on the lane.

III

Incessant night is born
perhaps from the dark table,
imperious center now
of dark, blind life.
Shadow draws nearer
very sharp remote places
and elastic it crosses
the so brief distance
from birth to nothing.
Then the word turns to stone
or diverges from behind
or is circularly delirious
or blurry and wasteland
and fleeting, fire
that ought to serve us
infinite nourishment.

Exiles

tras tanto acá y allá yendo y viniendo
       — Francisco de Aldana

They are here and there: passing by,
nowhere.
Each horizon: where an ember invites.
They could go toward any fissure.
No compass or voices.

They cross deserts that the hot sun
or frost burns
and limitless, infinite paddocks
turning them real,
that would make them almost of earth and pasture.

Their glance lies down like a dog,
without the tender recourse of wagging its tail.
Their glance lies down or draws back,
becomes dirt in the wind,
if no one returns it.
Does not revisit the blood or reach
whom it should.

It merely dissolves.

Still Canto

No matter the dazzling sun,
a minute after midday
it is already night,
for dark times impose
doubtful future clarity.
The world reveals treacherous, larval
traits, clouds the clear.
The channel overflows,
impiousness embraces you threateningly
and it is arduous
to gather any inheritance.
You scrape in your private end of an era:
blind history freezes.
How to be more when less reigns!
You keep in your hand then,
talisman, phylacteries,
not a pebble, a still canto
where your soul can ignite.

Cocoon

When you say: *words*
what space are you closing?
when you think: *slowly, you will soon arrive*
where?:
       when in shadow's tone
someone distantly murmurs:
                you burn walled-in,
it is the only thing you hear.

And not what it is made of
this frozen cocoon
woven around you,
exact augur of electricities,
good, bitter conductor.

To Burn, To Quiet

Y ardamos, y callemos, y campanas
— PABLO NERUDA

Without home, dog, bay,
to quiet, as to throw oneself, while
the anxious feast of the ephemeral other burns.
(Abominable I
of mambo and rumba, a Rambo I
climbing the poor province's weather vane
and raving glories and spinning alone,
suddenly.
              Not glimpsing the interrupted wind
moving from other towers, from other tall, distant
battlements.)

Then, why not, throw oneself
toward oblivion,
where among rocks the river roars
and gusts go over bark,
the world's dry bark
where we end up,
everything being annulled and repeated.
And to quiet and by chance
hear in the immense, interior field,
a sound of harmonizing bells.

The Lie

The borders of a country fly
whose false center is in us
who knows where we are.
North is in South,
East and West are jumbled,
South is lost in the haze
and within the most living is the lie.

Who doesn't have a lie cub?
Who doesn't give it its accustomed party,
imposing it in an imaginary field?
Who doesn't dredge or air
their minimal lie, gray or grandiose,
and take it to
where insects, birds fly,
real, each to their own?

And how many
watch over the other's lie
as they are innocently observed
by ever-honest death.

The Injured Man's Greeting

Save, silently.
You already know
what crosses will mark your grave,
crosses you have apparently already polished.
Their splinters do not allow you to forget
that, as you ought to, you haven't died.
Above all do not forget to not forget what kills,
what your mind occupies, the stain:
the vile disasters,
the distant motives,
the immobile formulas
in the inexactitude of histories.

A thorn is a thorn is a thorn
and it lasts much longer than the precarious rose.

Botánica

Here there is no rue, nothing of plants.
If perhaps Judas trees rising toward crimson,
kidnapped by the sun on the lonely sidewalks,
and evergreens:
                    situation of vegetal silence
because they say nothing or,
in their language dead to me,
these vicious ranks
I don't know what about a hospital they affirm,
reiterated and bluish.
But not one branch of rue, I say again.
No sweet acacia either.
                    Perhaps with great difficulty,
rosemary, fragrant ornamental shrub,
lasts in the garden,
attends to me with its aroma
of Venetian bread, of rapid train
but halted wheel
in memory for always,
like happiness that is not a sharp edge.

But not one rue plant.

Laurels

We will no longer go to the forest,
they cut down the laurels,
they cut down the cypresses,
the poplars, the oaks,
the civil palm trees,
the prudent araçuaria,   *araucaria*
the pine, the eucalyptus
after teaching them a lesson.

We will not go to the forest anymore,
in no place, where?,
if the desert prospers
more than weeds.
They cut down the laurels
air, hope,
they cut down the possible:
they cut down the cutable,

the clouds on high,
the rivers at their feet.
Our death ripens
with the death of fish.

San Miniato

All contrasts,
as disordered life,
yet beautiful, elegant,
San Miniato al Monte,
    almost
          in the air,
              beats
its feathered marble
toward the starry sky
and receives the secular steps
of imperfect poets.

What poetry keeps
of wretched and perverse,
the exterior searching for exterior,
vain glory and applause
even though it knows them to be inane,
was exalted here,
beneath the patterned ceiling,
among columns permitting
variety, beneath mosaics
of golden, flaming reds.
We said, we said,
but the flagstones name:
Elena Frosini, Enrico Petrai, Adolfo Targioni:
they can silence their history,
because they are, in their silence, eternal.
As the orbit our steps ignore,
where spins in its mystery
black and white,
the zodiac.

Stone, marble, mosaic, grating, cupola:
perfections more solid
than the short, dependent word.
It flies an instant and
like mist falls,
without becoming cloud
or feeding rivers.

There is no defect in things celestial
nor a wretched envy
that makes the gods ashamed
to present themselves before us*

Yet we, imperfect,
before this peace appear,
                    and disturb it.

* Gemistus Pletho

from *Reduction of the Infinite*

Parenthesis, Fragile Home

When dark skies worsen
open a parenthesis, tepid sign,
fragile home
having no more roof
than the imagined firmament
(even if it is austere, sour, ill-fated
if it is another who opens it),

think in two hands
protecting your face,
truly looking into you,
clusters sun against winter,
sun and human solvency.

Although you must cross
time's forests,
trample so many dry leaves
on memory's ground,
careful to not be swallowed
by ditches of surprising erosion,
find yourself in the parenthesis,
as in words always silent.

Culture of Palimpsest

Everything here is palimpsest,
palimpsest passion:

adrift,
        erase the little that has been done,
begin from nothing,
affirm drifting,
look at oneself among the increasing nothingness,
mind the toxic,
kill the healthy,
write delirious stories for the shipwrecked.

Careful:
the past is not lost without reprimand,
do not tread on air.

Sums

horse and knight are two animals

One plus one, we say. And we think:
one apple plus one apple,
one glass plus one glass,
always equal things.

What a change when
one plus one is a Puritan
plus a Gamelan,
a jasmine flower plus an Arab,
a nun and a cliff,
a canto and a mask,
once again a garrison and a damsel,
someone's hope
plus another's dream.

Slow Obstacles

If this afternoon's poem
were the mineral
falling toward a magnet
in a very deep shelter;

if it were a necessary fruit
for someone's hunger,
and hunger and poem
ripened punctually;

if it were the bird living for its wing,
if it were the wing sustaining the bird,
if nearby there were an ocean
and twilight gulls' cry
marked the awaited hour;

if my word kept emerald
today's ferns
—not those where time upholds fossils—
if everything were natural and friendly…

But unsure itineraries
disseminate without exact sense.
We have become nomads,
without splendor in the journey
or direction within the poem.

Salamanders' Mail

E vieni
tu pure voce prigioniera
. . . voce di sangue, persa e resituita
alla mia sera.
       — EUGENIO MONTALE

Salamanders' mail,
from the cold to fire
how much flight, voyage
distance.
Now one burns when foretelling
and at the edge of water, of arrival,
what fire, what endless
embracing ways of scruples,
so much ceremonial suspense
inclined to empty pillows
and the plates perhaps disposed
swallowing comparative hours.

Crossing a pernicious vapor
desolated voices come,
asking for help and company
and innocent, to the window
panting from breathlessness,
they arrive unhurt, luminous
and for echoless word
and friendships without more friends
they spread with their quiet pain
a soft wing of bandage.

Someone still plants in time
the backyard's cinerarias,
for me they ascend stairs
that go to a sky barely belonging
and in roof-top dawns

on my behalf they keep looking for,
always, that crazy gray rabbit
that knew to leave his prison
and flees secretly since then,
each day in the bareness I cry.

We veil our constancy
so it does not seem tears;
happiness like mouthfuls of bread,
magnified, they become diamonds.
Midnight's trench
of possessed dogs,
and sorrow's lesson
that in air's smoke remains
like the day's fallen leaves
we winnow all inventory.

How much longer?
But was it truth shared?

                                        1975–1985

Annunciation

The angel in satin comes, wings retracted,
to the terrace's corner where,
at the foot of the column,
the virgin read the book now forgotten.
A pup, next to her,
raises a restless paw, while
against twilight,
from the angel's warning finger
you could say a thread starts
and a docile hand folds
over a startled chest.
The colors
are those that Veronese uses:
wine's dregs Mary's gown,
dark blue her cloak.
The sky in the twilight advances
from an intense azure to pink shreds,
announcing for tomorrow,
a storm perhaps.
But a slight gray veil
now curdles over things
that ignore
how destiny will be read.

Everything occurs at an abysmal distance
from this world,
that still imagines itself free
from Beast and Limit.

The Glory of Philitis

Philitis, Egyptian shepherd, plowed nothing.
He was poor.
He did not intuit a new boat
of surer, more beautiful lines.
Did not imagine gardens
or sketches or music,
he left nothing written,
did not move a figure from the sacred profile.

He only took his beasts to pasture
at the foot of hills
where Chephren and Cheops,
abominable kings,
for half a century,
raised their tombs
over the shoulders of exhausted peoples.

The latter, hating their rulers,
did not want to name them.
Justly they said
to speak of these sites:
—There
by the pyramids of Philitis.

To Arms

for Ernesto Mejía Sánchez

Your life spent in longing for your homeland,
cursing Somoza,
in the impatience of banishment
and friendship's stillness.
You lost so much,
except for your solar condition
and grace, which was more than solar,
intermingled with reluctance
and syntax with dance and rupture.
One brash, intoxicated day
you stole a stone from us—Rodocrosita and silver—
falling down laughing,
while you said love love
to bewitch us,
with a lure on each e,
placing in front of eyes
hand and heart of tin
of an innocent ring:
now, fixed, absurd spider web
over the memory's dispersed gold.
Blue flies pass
over wise inventions and flight's ravings:
from there the Rodocrosita, the reasonably-priced ring,
the roof where your sister the nun was distracted,
your body's invisible pile of bones
and *Tzitzipandacuri 2* with its alcohol glass.

Against their stele rest
your arms, your poems.

Order of Angels

To Susana Chaer
To Susana Garbino de Saráchaga

A precarious economy of angels,
two or three,
         no more.
                But they suffice.
They place fluid fingers
in the hodgepodge,
oil in the shipwreck,
to begin,
        a smile over chaos.

When they move away
a very soft color remains stretched
over this irregular map
that I would not want to lose,
that the fortunate heart recognizes.

Lunatic Solo, Legitimate Isolation

3

Tenacious glorious days
against truth fable
and the soul squares us,
tenacious glorious days.
Yet stony homes
with their ways of not seeing you,
conceal an inert
variation of severity.
Remains of consciousness say:
is not silence your fate?

4

Of ambushes and errors
will be born a map of nuisances
where the bears dance
to the sound of old errors.
A terrace of pain
contemplates hopelessly
the balance's doubts.
Could it be that the light enjoys
mistaking the path
the naïve dare to take.

from *Byobu's ABCs*

A Story

There is a story. When it started is not exactly known. Those who could be connected to the story actually ignore that it exists. It doesn't have a name to identify it and it's unclear whether it has one or two protagonists. It could be A's story that B doesn't accept or vice-versa. It could also be that neither know that the story exists or concerns them. It's entirely possible that one could die without knowing he's the real protagonist of the story and the other has taken his place. In any case, a story's existence, even if it's not well-defined and attributed, even if it's only in the stage of constitution, barely latent, spreads emanations in an imprecise but urgent way. Byobu, who suspects his dark existence, feels obligated to scrutinize like a philatelic the edges of his possible apparition. It's not about underestimating the disordered, flexible density: at any moment it can acquire an oriented speed that lowers over him its unbreathable marasmus. Because many dream of the adventure that ought to hatch for them each day. But when it appears, they perceive some defect, even the signs of a terrifying leprosy upon its supposedly tempting appearance. And they feign ignorance, although they don't forget the disregarded call. Yet the story remains free, unworried. Like a lightening bolt that no lightning rod can halt. And Byobu knows he is the exposed par excellence. And so he watches closely, untrusting, the stories wandering freely, without A or B to accept them.

Very Platonic Love

He loves the sun. He can't live without the sun. He flees from it. He knows that on the other side of the sidewalk, where the oppressively white house is, there is also the oasis beneath the evergreen, for a measured time, as long as autumn doesn't arrive to save him from the disintegration that summer threatens him with. Parcels of crows, in spite of their blackness that seems everything-proof, suddenly no longer resist. Crystallized, they fracture, free to its fate the green material organized under different names, less perishable than it. Successive mirages sparkle and are extinguished, breaking the variable distances on the road that Byobu should have traveled, yes, if not obligated to stop at the sweet shadow's shelter, from there to spy on the sun, before which he feels crushed, and without which he wouldn't know how to live.

Knots

Byobu concludes that he ought to begin by ending. To end mediating among disasters, trying to temper the trepidations of trolleys, whose trajectories ignore him. He ought to give up tepid, disastrous transactions. Leave behind limbos. Ignore everything that the iniquitous initiated. Close, close, close: dark skies approach, gratings sing, showy, vertically striping the repeated landscape. Everything converges to generate the cage, to which Byobu ought to adjust, if he doesn't begin, precisely, by ending. He has discovered that the custom of looking straight ahead, just as walking straight ahead, lays traps of rope. And for each rope there is never just one hand willing to pull. He imagines a theory of periods. But it's already known. Many periods united are transformed to ellipses. Then, must he foresee a definitive suspension of his running horizon? Knots, periods, rope, magnitudes reduced, disasters.

Anguish

Byobu's anguish aggressively threatens. Liquid, leaking, it takes up everything around him. At times, solid, dry, it invades the holes surrounding him like sand. It grows within itself, liquid or dry. It is natural, then, that his breath is cutoff, as if a hereditary disease were at the point of being let loose.

He goes out to walk, to leave that weight behind, under wind's power, covered and confused with a shadow. It entails an empty being walking through an empty city beneath an empty sky. A decisive empty silence envelopes him. Perhaps one thinks that silence is always there. One has not heard the marvelous plenitude of generous silences. Oppression expresses itself from time to time in terrible formulas unable to replace or annul. Supposing that the unexpected words of others could dominate it, he walks toward the public library, searching for those enclosed in books. The world's restlessness welcomes him: each book holds a different form of uneasiness, malaise, sickness or pain that asks: Isn't my case the worst? Each one — soul struggling to save itself, hostage rescued provisionally by the hand that has chosen him — calls out with delicious recourses, tempting and distinct. And Byobu gives in, rarely enters in others' happiness and in the end finds himself liberated from his own asphyxia, less grave than some he has half-seen. It has not been a magical operation: he has learned to minimize himself.

from *Trema*

Task

Open word by word the wasteland,
open ourselves and look toward the signifying aperture,
suffer to work the coal's place
later to extinguish it and ease the burnt one's moans.

Calculated Error

Deep sea words
every instant surge to die
by the hundreds, contaminated fish.
They do not help one another,
they fear the risk, die,
do not know what they know.
Does whoever loves and shelters them
free them from the silence
placing them among oblivion
and imprisoned magic?
Does one play with more danger?

A gust wanders through the afternoon.
It follows the light swell:
may your enthusiasm
not give in to the retained canto.

Arrows

To witness phrases shot
as if said by beings
who speak alone beside the seashore,
sure that no one hears
(and the water would burn
to accept or refuse them).

Who pass each other
as if beneath a desert gust,
instantly covered with sand
immobilizing them.
And they remain on the riddles'
fringe to resolve
on the last afternoon,
when you already knew it and so burn the sails.

Last Night of Some Year

After the clean day
in the awaiting night arose,
spotless in its only sign,
the rocketry of uniform joy.
The small flash barely grazed
night's silent carpets
before dying,
as if isolated, it too,
from the distant celebration.
Did it aspire to be alone
so sure of itself?

Is all hope morbid?

On the Back of the Sky

It is not chance
what occurs because of fate:
a fragment of nothing is protected
from not being, it mixes
with signs, impulses,
yeses and nos, delays and advances,
traces of celestial geometry,
rapid coordinates in time
and something occurs.
Loops for us pallid
are obvious for what we don't see,
and we the open window
from which the white cloth flies
covered in patterns.
Yet we call fate
our insufficient imagination.

The Visible God

We had taken our leave of the sun
and suddenly a window opens in the sky:
among two shreds of cloud
it appears of fragile color
with a distinct light.
Something happened behind those curtains.
Does it warn that perhaps tomorrow
we should not await it?
That the rising ozone
will render it our enemy?

Do not shipwreck yet.
Three yellow awnings
refute faith's damage.
May that blessing,
another hope
also weigh on you.

If Blind

If sky, if blue, if blind,
beneath a sun of suns,
silence.
Distant colloquial clouds feign
the unforeseeable arabesque
that life imposes on your life.
Do not anticipate more dreams, look
in the distance, that high, convex bird
searching for another boundary, shade.

No Saga

No saga will grant words
to the unborn child
because his mother lies pierced,
nor to the terrified mute
without canto before the tenacious tank,
nor to the blind man groping in smoke's night.

Forests burn and the desert is delirious
and the milky river for nocturnal dreams.
Not even one tree of fragile music
will cover the tragedy of the always conquered,
secret as the center of coal.

Yet it will never be for obtuse triumph.
Once more,
defeat will be called honor,
even though triumph's rumble conceals it.

Fortune

For years, to enjoy the error
and its amendment,
to be able to speak, walk freely,
not exist mutilated,
enter churches or not,
read, listen to beloved music,
at night to be as during the day.

To not be married in arrangement,
measured in goats,
suffer the rule of relatives
or legal stoning.
To no longer march
nor admit words
that place in blood
iron filings.
To discover for yourself
another being unexpected
on glance's bridge.

To be human and woman, nothing more nothing less.

The Street

Por fin había dado con una calle de un solo minuto . . .

—Jacobo Fijman

It didn't resist. make a fuss (interrupt)

It did not throw its room on its back. *wtf*
It was going to be a garden,
they wanted it a fortress.
From no one expect nothing. *??*
It doesn't expect anything from anyone . .

With its bunches of flowers in the air
lightly moving
it waves a silent goodbye
to what is happening and leaves.

complete
South and North do not make
the meeting with street's
vague destiny,
swift with parallel lines.
impatient   grid?

Nominal creature,
knows how to keep phantoms,
voices becoming smoke
without the eye opening them.

Grounded, supine
Terrified, with its back turned,
the street unfolds
into the other floating
among wells and skies.
between   pools?

Yes, spring comes,
yet the grey knows
that its profound place →*depth*
cannot give flowers.

It cannot, no, it cannot? — or step
And the passage with love,
lone sorrows that in you
are sown, can do nothing?

Bogota, 2001

Beneath smoky clouds, without conviction,
awry, the rain falls.
There are yellow blossoms dense with gray waters
and pines, pines, pines and flocks.
The eucalyptus, those with red flowers,
have settled on the green, irreducible earth.
Everything knows it's safe in its own color
and awaits spring's kite
rising with the winds.
Nothing is disturbed if poetry lasts.
Is it nourished by the world's silence?

New Certainties

Poetry
does not indulge history,
tell stories;
The listener
does not dialogue
with more words than patience.
Poetry is not caricature or caryatid.
It never appeared.
It dies, in an indelicate air,
chrematistically organized.

Project of a son
running behind a father
whose voice would suckle him?
A hurried person's train?
Better deserted harbor,
abandoned platform.

Merry-Go-Round

The carrousel, roundabout, the what
was its name, merry-go-round, calls
me offering a deer, a buggy,
a swan and reared-up horse,
the prodigy turning round so serenely,
so serenely trotting through the air
with organ and chimes,
breeze not moving the horse's tail
white and golden, yet danger,
danger of falling in full flight,
of falling and being almost forgotten
by father, to get off at a different spot
than getting on and being alone,
cloudless, no longer wind in my hair,
lost without the delicious horror
of flying with hands seizing
the mane that frees me and I clay
in air's oven recuperating
its serene, original form,
alone and wingless.

Courtesies

That venerable past,
someone else's or hardly mine in any way,
in a box it was kept
for years. Where now?

Slow snapshots
sought to detain the moment
wind beats or watch disciplines;
against the sea, on stones
like sleeping whales' shoulders,
hands save great hats
from flying to the foam,
prudent weights of
long skirts reinforce.

Still the secular courtesy
of a pose reigns:
head resting in a hand,
elbow on a meaningless column,
in sight the prestige of a book
and a curtain fabling.

And there are smiles, undoubtedly,
among words of friendly scansion
and anonymous children growing
in suits of such brief Sundays
and to someone will go their fabric prisons.

That past still precipitates blood,
acuminated rumor
for which there are no celebrated ears.
Upon tomb oblivions

and indifferences that some disposed,
a swayed perfume.
How to avoid it from being dust without consequence
in my suddenly useless memory.

Riches

She kept white papers,
beautiful buttons of lucky dresses,
photographs of faces without names:
safe-conducts to cross the bridge.

Yet she found emptiness
or sequences of atrocious syllables,
names with lost faces,
bits of vague sensations,
ways without marvel,
an intrusion of nuisance
in memory's flavor.

Recollections without good sense,
old or recent,
intimate,
        excessive,
dark,
     pendular,
spun like free dervishes

and something they have in common:
they are from inside borders.

On the Dark Porch

The very you you grazed,
the one who will never be
in the little that is left,
the one who wanted to have been
and a sum of splintered instances
of life separated
from undoubtedly dreams:
How certain among uncertainty?
No longer keys: whiteness
and epidermis more or less exposed.
And a grotto silence
beneath the strident forest.
You dreamt in the bewitched clearing
in the center of the dark tangle,
in the intact guides and marks
and the porch all light.
This a return
to the beginning,
to the unfractured voice.
To happy, irrational certainty.

Return Trip

To regress is
to be concerned once more
with returning to earth
the last months' dust;
receive from the world
sleeping mail;
attempt to know
how long
a dove's memory lasts.

Also
to recognize yourself
as just another bee
that is for the hive, barely
a unity buzzing.
This, just one more bee,
very dispensable.

Perhaps an Explanation

Someone leaves to not go,
to remain encapsulated
in an imaginary past,
wasteland of never forget.

Someone can understand beneath another sky
how a bird gives thanks,
wick's slow force
and returning to constancy.

Dissolved, extinct, lies
evil's way become,
where men like trunks,
surrender their dreams, only float.

Even dead, many are obstacles,
gods with doses of venom.
Yet in a reflection
a small sun is kept. Everlasting flower.

Milan Café

These voices do not raise columns:
fragile stores float
without further ado abandoned.
No one of those seated here
dreamt of sharing a table with a tree
or spy the lineage of clouds,
their diaphanous coming and going.

This is not a place to remain:
you are not from this city, this country
this crepitating continent.
You know well the plot:
an indecisive, tense candle,
for more than a century,
declaring undeniable burden
and inventing nostalgias,
chained you to other places,
other violence, other prizes.
To a virgin, repeated history
that in vain you foresee.
And lament.

Closing

From everywhere the siblings leave:
Octavio one day, Tito on time
and here Laura and Amalia.
Living dead erased the others.
Opaque fringe trembles upon lengthening
in a dim sketch
and the solitary swallow passes by
and sky's lid has withered
and I go walking
suddenly toward the wonder I do not believe in.

Mining the Wall

Time's mission: confront the wall,
mine it, unknot its solid moorings,
temper its edge. Control your impatience:
one breath returns as a storm.

A twilight behind the Batoví
appears, bloodily splendid.
In your heart there must be ashes:
there is blood, still.

Existance: comes with flight or bushes,
a branch for glass and a smile
or stony terrain silence. Then, wall.

Gratitude

I thank my homeland for its errors,
those committed, those to come,
active, blind to its white mourning.
I thank the contrary gale,
the semi-forgetfulness, the spiny border of sophistry,
the fallacious denial of a dark gesture.
Yes, thank you, thank you very much
for having taken me to wander
so the hemlock has its effect
and it no longer hurts when
the metaphysical animal of absence*
bites

* Peter Sloterdijk

Lightning Source UK Ltd.
Milton Keynes UK
UKHW040108311218
334744UK00001B/49/P